The Conflict Resolution Library™

Dealing with Being the Oldest Child in Your Family

• Elizabeth Vogel •

The Rosen Publishing Group's

PowerKids Press™

New York

For my big sister, Cassie.

Published in 2000 by The Rosen Publishing Group, Inc.
29 East 21st Street, New York, NY 10010

Photo Credits and Photo Illustrations: pp. 4,8,12,16,19,20 © Andrea Levy; p. 7 © Skjold Photography; p. 11 © Ira Fox; p. 15 © Thomas Mangieri.

First Edition

Layout and design: Erin McKenna

#ENF 1-19-01

Vogel, Elizabeth.
   Dealing with being the oldest child in your family / by Elizabeth Vogel.
        p.   cm. — (The conflict resolution library)
   Includes index.
   Summary: Describes some of the responsibilities and privileges that come with being the oldest child in a family and offers advice on how to deal with both.
   ISBN 0-8239-5409-9 (lib. bdg.)
   1. Birth order—Psychological aspects—Juvenile literature. 2. First-born children—Psychology—Juvenile literature. 3. Sibling rivalry—Juvenile literature.
[1. Birth order. 2. Brothers and sisters.]　I. Title. II. Series.
   BF723.B5V64 1998
   155.9'24—dc21
                                  98-46439
                                  CIP
                                  AC

Manufactured in the United States of America

Contents

1 When You Are the Oldest 5
2 Brothers and Sisters 6
3 Your Own Time 9
4 Alexa and Her Brothers 10
5 The Lemonade Stand 13
6 Trouble with Siblings 14
7 Doing Things First 17
8 Juan's Job 18
9 Your Parents and You 21
10 Proud to Be the Oldest 22
   Glossary 23
   Index 24

When You Are the Oldest

Are you the oldest child in your family? If so, you have at least one younger brother or sister. You may even have lots of younger **siblings**. As the oldest child, you have an important role in your family. Your parents may ask you to help take care of your siblings. Maybe you help them with their homework. Maybe you teach them how to play games. Your siblings may ask you for your advice, since you are older and more **experienced**. Being the oldest can be a big **responsibility**.

◀ *As the oldest child, you are very important to your younger sibling.*

Brothers and Sisters

If you are the oldest child in your family, it was just you and your parents for a while. Then a sibling came along and your family changed. Sometimes you might find it hard to share your parents' attention. However, most of the time, you may find it fun to have younger siblings. They can be your friends and playmates. You are there for one another in good times and bad. Your siblings will also understand what it's like to be part of your family. They know how often you have spaghetti for dinner!

Siblings are not only relatives, they can be good friends, too. ▶

Your Own Time

Your younger siblings may look up to you and admire you. They may love to spend time with you. This can be fun, but sometimes you might want time for yourself. Maybe you want to read a book or watch your favorite show on television. Maybe you want to play with your friend from school. Your little sister might feel sad because she wants to play with you, too. You can explain that sometimes you can play with her, but sometimes you may need to do something else.

 This boy enjoys some quiet time on his own with a favorite book.

Alexa and Her Brothers

Alexa came home from school to find her little brothers, Theo and Shawn, waiting to play with her. Alexa couldn't play with them because she had some friends over. The boys looked disappointed. Later, Alexa went to see her brothers in the backyard. She told them, "I'm sorry. Sometimes I need time with just my friends, but I still love you. Maybe we can play together tomorrow." The boys gave Alexa a hug. They felt better knowing their older sister cared about them even if they couldn't always play with her.

Alexa made sure her brothers knew she loved them even if she was playing with someone else. ▶

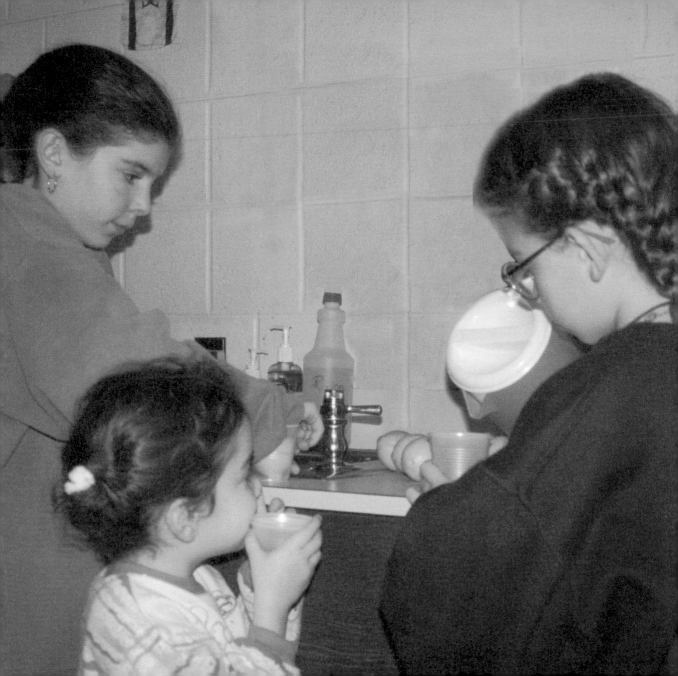

The Lemonade Stand

Eva had a great idea. "Let's make a lemonade stand!" she said to her younger sisters, Sandy and Sharon. Eva showed Sharon how to squeeze the lemons into the pitcher. She taught Sandy how to mix in the water and the sugar. Soon all three sisters were selling delicious lemonade to friends in the neighborhood. "You always have the best ideas, Eva," said Sharon. Eva felt proud that she was able to lead her sisters in a fun activity. She loved to teach her little sisters new and exciting things.

As the oldest child in your family, you can teach your siblings many things.

Trouble with Siblings

Sometimes you might **argue** with your siblings. This is because you disagree about something, and then you get angry. Tell your sibling how you feel. Listen to his feelings, too. Figure out a way to **compromise**. This means you both give in a little. You can teach your sibling how to compromise. Maybe you want to play video games but your little brother would rather play a board game. You can work it out so that you play one video game and then play one board game. That way everyone can be happy.

Instead of fighting, try to work things out when you don't get along. ▶

Doing Things First

Sometimes it's hard to be the oldest. You might have more responsibilities, like babysitting for your siblings, or helping to clean the house. However, you might also get to do some fun things because you are older. You might be the first to go to sleepover parties or to go camping with a friend's family. It might be hard on your siblings, who are not allowed to do the same things as you. You can tell them that one day they will be able to do these special things, too. It will be worth the wait!

◀ *Older siblings can sometimes do fun things that younger siblings aren't allowed to do yet, like go to sleepovers.*

Juan's Job

Juan had to clean the kitten's litter box. Juan thought this was unfair. He does so much more than his brothers. Juan takes the garbage out and helps wash the dishes. Juan's parents explained that he is old enough to help at home, but he is also old enough to do more exciting things, like go to the amusement park. Juan's brothers don't do as many chores, but they are too young to go to the park. Juan thought about the rides and the cotton candy. Maybe cleaning the kitty mess wasn't so bad after all.

Being older means you're ready to help around the house. ▶

Your Parents and You

It's important to set aside some special time to spend with your parents. You can tell them about your day. You might have a problem and need their help. You can tell them about something you did well. Maybe you want to tell your parents about how you did on your spelling test. Maybe you are trying out for the school play. Your parents love to hear how you are doing. You are their first child and they want to know all about you.

Proud to Be the Oldest

Joey walked his sister to school. His parents **trusted** him to make sure she arrived safely. When they got to school, Joey brought his sister to her class and said goodbye. He felt proud that he had done his job right. Doing his job well made Joey feel grown-up and **confident**. Maybe he would be able to take on more responsibilities at home. Joey liked being the oldest. You can feel proud of all that you can do as the oldest child, just like Joey.

Glossary

argue (AR-gyoo) When people who don't agree about something get angry with each other.

compromise (KOM-pruh-myz) When people give up part of what they want to come to an agreement.

confident (KON-fih-dent) A firm belief in oneself and one's abilities.

experience (ik-SPIR-ee-ents) To have knowledge or skill gained by doing something or seeing things.

responsibility (ree-spon-sih-BIH-lih-tee) Something, such as a chore, that a person must do.

sibling (SIB-ling) A person's sister or brother.

trust (TRUST) To be able to depend on someone.

Index

A
argue, 14
attention, 6

C
chores, 17, 18
compromise, 14
confident, 22

E
experience, 5

F
families, 6
   role in, 5
feelings, 9, 10,
   14
   of pride, 13, 22
friends, 6, 9, 10,
   13, 17
fun, 6, 9, 13, 17

P
parents, 5, 6, 18,
   21, 22

R
responsibilities, 5,
   17, 22

S
siblings, 5, 6, 17
   disagreeing with,
   14
   teaching, 5, 13
   who admire you,
   9

T
time
   for yourself, 9
   with parents, 21
trust, 22